A View of Buildings and Water

GEOFFREY O'BRIEN was born in New York City. His poetry has been collected previously in *A Book of Maps*, *The Hudson Mystery*, and *Floating City: Selected Poems 1978–1995*. He is also the author of a number of prose works including *Hardboiled America*, *Dream Time: Chapters from the Sixties*, *The Phantom Empire*, *The Browser's Ecstasy*, and *Castaways of the Image Planet*. He is editor-in-chief of The Library of America.

A View of Buildings and Water

GEOFFREY O'BRIEN

SALT

PUBLISHED BY SALT PUBLISHING
PO Box 202, Applecross, Western Australia 6153
PO Box 937, Great Wilbraham, Cambridge PDO CB1 5JX United Kingdom

© Geoffrey O'Brien, 2002

The right of Geoffrey O'Brien to be identified as the
author of this work has been asserted by him in accordance
with Section 77 of the Copyright, Designs and Patents Act 1988.

First published 2002

Printed and bound in the United Kingdom by Lightning Source

Typeset in Swift 9.5 / 13

ISBN 1 876857 55 2 paperback

SP

1 3 5 7 9 8 6 4 2

For Michael O'Brien

Contents

Acknowledgments

Some of these poems appeared originally in *The Literary Review*, *Good Foot*, *Talisman*, *Angle*, *New American*, *The KGB Bar Book of Poems*, and *110 Stories: New York Writes After September 11*. "Heads in Limbo" was written to accompany an exhibition of sculptures by Susan Mastrangelo at the Locus Gallery, New York City, in 2000; a collaborative edition of it, combining art and text, has been published on-line by Art Resources Transfer (artretran.com). The writing of these poems was made possible in part by a gift from The Fund for Poetry.

Part I

For a Diva

You can be anything. Zenobia of Palmyra
startled awake in childhood by a bird
in her father's palace almost floats into the courtyard.
The cook whose boyfriend's been hauled to prison
for killing her mother writes letters never delivered
because the landlord wants to control her life, waits in the hall
to assault her when she comes back from shopping. The
        bourgeois wife
sleeps with her husband's banker and having given birth
to a foundling who grows up to be a semiliterate stick-up artist
must finally recognize it's her own child who's stabbed her
from the mark on his wrist. The hermit lady in the hills
has dreams of fire. Between silver pools the pampered hostess
poses for her guests. In the most dimly-lit of after-hours dives
the disinherited kidnap victim sings bawdy laments.

The world is a mask. Lakes are moved from one place to another
and cars enter the city just as the shop lights go on
so that one form of glitter can lose itself in another.
How many years have you been looking out the window
practicing the expression, half of regret and half of cruelty,
that the others will notice when they come back from their
        excursion
and walk into the sitting room unannounced? Nobody
        recognizes
whose gesture yours most resembles. It takes years of language
        study
to disguise so expertly a pattern of kinship. The tragedy of
        waiting,
the tragedy of being bored, the tragedy of no longer knowing
how late the local train runs, these are things that can dissolve
as easily as dusk becomes twilight into the contrast
between the neglected lawn and the fountain that still waters it
at a point when even the servants have given up on appearances.

But to try on a new outfit: nothing can compare to it, the joy
of that first time. It's like destroying the world
so as to demonstrate that it was a window display
held over into the wrong season. Now the spring comes
and we can take our rings off, as if ornament after all
had never been more than an extension of nudity. The dance
          pavilion
reaches its peak of attractiveness before anyone arrives. What
          splendor
wastes away in the unexamined hours when the local dignitaries
are still sleeping, the crates not yet pried open, is a fit subject
for the wordless song that takes shape as your fingers
play over the keyboard, untutored but prescient.
That was when the house was really a house, or an anticipation
of the hour when it will be a house again. From the cold hills
must be where this breeze came from, only slightly tempered.

Because everything is malleable. You already knew that
from looking at the paints and powders on the dressing table
in the forbidden gallery. Robbers can hide behind curtains
with no more difficulty than a doctor writing a prescription
for a sleeping drug or a nursemaid exceeding her authority
by leaving the baby alone while she consorts with a corporal.
You didn't decide to forget your name any more than you
          decided
that today would be a good day for taking the skiff out
to explore the lake's uninhabited shore and get a look at what's
          left
of the burnt-out fortifications. To find yourself on the water at
          noon
 is like emerging from the coma after a carriage accident.
The sun blinds you to where you came from. Whose idea was it
to build the dock so far from the house that it would have
          required a special trip
to see that the rope was dangling there as if deliberately
          unfastened?

[4]

To be a foreigner in your own countryside, or to forget
where you buried the swaddling clothes that would clear up
once and for all the identity of your child's father, are
    inconveniences
that not even a change of name can altogether resolve.
When shadows become complicated, deny everything.
There are always the mountains. If you insist on revenge
they will fail to understand, but you must insist anyway.
Just as no one can measure the delight of peeking
over your lover's shoulder at a gilt book of poems
retrieved from the ancestral library, no one can begin to imagine
how long it might take for the dispersal of the sunlight
you were reading by to register as not simply a betrayal of honor
but a theft of identity. When you come back you will stare at
    them
until they feel themselves start to become invisible.

Voice Over

(ghost aria for Edmond O'Brien)

Suddenly it all started
        to fall into place. It was like being
            shaken out of a doped-up pipe dream
where everything looked like
        some crazy modern painting,
            the streets and faces twisted into the wrong ratio.
I was wide awake
        and it felt like being wide awake
        for the first time in my life,
only for me that was the same as being
        in the middle of a nightmare.
        But I felt a weird relief
even as I realized just how thoroughly I'd been had.
        I could almost convince myself
        that maybe now it was a new ball game,
maybe the tables were about to turn.
        I was finally playing with a full deck
        instead of the stack of jokers they'd handed me.
A frame-up: that's what it had been from the start,
        and I was the sap it was made to order for.
        It was a beaut, all right,
with me as the fall guy
        wrapped up neatly and tied with pink ribbons.
        They must have busted a gut laughing
while they watched me stroll into their trap.
        The trail I thought I'd tumbled to
        just on account of being such a sharpie
had been mapped out long before I turned the corner.
        It might as well have been signposted
        Suckers Enter Here, or maybe
Frame Job Next Right. I thought I'd written
        the book on frame-ups, and here I turned out
        to be the main character, Exhibit A
right in the center ring. It was a story line

constructed by a con guy with so many angles
he made Einstein look like a dummy.
I'd been on a losing streak since page one
and the last chapter was death. I'd been sweet-talked
straight into the slaughterhouse.
Every move I'd made
had been strictly according to plan—
their plan. They'd cased me so well
they knew just how I'd trip myself up.
Me, the wise guy,
the guy that was too smart and too tough
ever to fall for a set-up like that.
Sure, just like Adam
wouldn't ever have sold himself short
for a taste of homegrown apple. Just like Samson
was too cute an operator to let himself get taken
for the price of a cheap haircut.
It was the oldest game in the world,
played for the same old stakes,
a dame in mink with eyes a mile deep
and a bundle of money
that couldn't have been planted more obviously
if they'd labeled it Please Take Me.
I'd swallowed the bait
and now they had their hooks in so deep
I'd have to rip myself to shreds
if I ever wanted to break free of their racket.
And maybe that was the way it had to be.
Maybe this was the sucker they'd choke on.
They'd cut the cards,
now they could live with the shuffle.
It was downright comical if you thought about it.
We were all going to have a good laugh before we burned.
Say, if this is when we cash the chips
let's do it in style.
They'd get me, all right, I was gone,
I already knew that it was check-out time
in the luxury-class neon hotel

where nobody ever checks back in.
But for some customers the price is always higher
than they want to pay. This is hell, isn't it?
Hey buddy, they tell me in these parts
the coin of the realm
is a man's life and breath
and the spare change is his everlasting soul.
This is when I start to feel good.
The city dawn is barging into the side streets
and I'm starting to feel almost human again
when I think about how it will be
finally to call in every last IOU.

Virgilian Herb

(for Devin Dougherty)

The sun is fringed with heat loss.

∾

It escapes from its canyon.

∾

Black cities.
The well of forgetting.

∾

The water has a shape
As it hurls itself down the terraced path.

∾

Leafwork.
The terraced face
Gliding from the conical storehouse.

∾

The dried ash
Traps light in its gutters.
Armies of clouds do ceremonial battle.

∾

After the floods
The new growth
Forces a road through the highway.

∾

The travelers who came from the Water City
Were the inventors of music.

~

A stringed instrument shaped like a bridge
Describes the hiding places
Where they burrow into the splices.

~

A rift carved in dirt.
The grooves where the pebbles almost touch
Deflect light
From the accidental tunnels.

~

Here a wall burned.

~

The wads of crushed sticks
Stand for what the dead remember.
The seams of vine leaves
Mimic the chapters of the lost book.

~

Here it taught
How the coast was rescued from downpour,
Here how the interpreter
Entered the body of a mite
And crept into the soil
To keep vigil at the root tips.

~

There were twelve books—
The Book of Oak, the Book of Cobweb,
The Book of Gum, the Book of Omen,
The Book of Sluice, the Book of Famine,
The Book of Bone, the Book of Smoke,
The Book of Bells, the Book of Footsteps,
The Book of Sandstone and the Book of Night—
Until they fell apart from disuse.

≈

After language has been buried for a long time
Moss breaks out among the scratches.
In its moist tomb
The dead name sprouts.

Peninsula

In the ruins of Pyongyang
Leatherbound volumes

Of Voltaire and Diderot,
Printed in the eighteenth century,

Are passed from hand to hand
As textbooks for the open air schools

Where among rusted cans and hoarded bottle caps
Venerable half-blind teachers

Give vocabulary lessons. Here is the spine,
The mind, the eye. The cloth fiber of the pages

Endures well in the dry sunlight
Of the northern desert. The letters burn

Like little black stars
On a screen of sand. The diagram of reason,

Branching and skeletal, pokes out into cuplike appendages
Bearing the labels Justice and Growth and Energy.

Strong as preserved venom,
And as life-giving, the forms of the letters

Blink against the continental weather mass
And spell out absently the name of Mongolia.

Heads in Limbo

(for Susan Mastrangelo)

"Who is who and who
isn't who"—I croon myself to sleep
from the moment I wake.

～

From the secrecy of my left eye
I watch the neighbors
without risking a word.

～

I would have told you all about it
but in your haste
you neglected to arrive.

～

What would my life have been
without the burden of the clouds
to unsettle the morning?

～

The end came
just as I was enjoying
yet another fresh start.

～

At the risk of seeming intrusive
I have occasionally been so bold
as to look out.

~

For so long I sat
staring at the world
that my face became a mask.

~

Confronted with a dead end
all I can say is
don't get me started.

~

So much has been hidden
that the time has come
to wait for the right moment.

~

What you think you see
is what isn't visible
except when you look away.

~

I took my time
getting up, and now the grass
is obscured by sunlight.

~

It's never easy,
least of all when
you think it isn't.

~

That we should be grateful
even for what we didn't get
is not such a bad credo, is it?

~

All the day through
I see, I see, without a care
for what I look like doing it.

~

It would have been better
to come at a different time
and now it's too late to leave.

~

The world is so simple
that my face
has not one wrinkle.

~

Watch out
and you may avoid
what is in fact inevitable.

~

Catastrophe
always seemed a pretty word
and somehow still does.

～

On the first day of school
I was as I am now:
how delightful.

～

All the same
it's better to weigh your words
before remaining silent.

～

The wind howls around me
until I have the pleasure of feeling
like a ruined archaic statue.

～

There are games
so intricately delicious
that not even their rules can be published.

～

Nothing here will hurt you
and if it does
you can go back from whence you came.

～

It's so wild here
I've forgotten why
I didn't get invited sooner.

~

Nothing like the satisfaction
of composing one's features
to relish the satisfaction of nothing.

~

Keep a sharp eye
on the periphery while savoring
the lantern show in the middle.

~

There is a tale so dark
that even if I told it
you would not remember.

~

If you don't know
what I'm looking at
keep it to yourself.

~

No care, not a hair
misplaced, I told myself
all the way here.

~

World, you're a picturesque vista
I can close the blinds on
anytime I please.

~

Really, that last bit, the
elegant one that just turned
the corner, was worth the ticket.

~

So surprised
to find myself here
that nothing since has surprised me.

~

Do you think anybody noticed
when I stopped thinking
about where I was?

~

It's just too slippery
when a glance
is the solidest thing around.

~

Think how cunningly
even strangers can be disguised
by my new wraparound glasses.

~

All was calm until
one day when I blinked
the sky cracked.

~

Who do you think
this is, anyway?
And who wants to know?

The Prophet

You stepped out of a frame, or more properly
out of a framed image in a store specializing
in images from a variety of periods, early Egyptian,
late Rococo, the advent of the talkies. Wherever
people have an urge to stand framed in doorways,
to let strings of beads drape them, wherever they feel free
to choreograph a dance interpretive of a windstorm,
that's where I'll find you. Your bedroom is splashed
with mythological scenes, your radio hums with polka music.
In the lost history of the world, the one whose revolutions
were achieved without ceremonial burnings, you play the role
of the prophet who on second thought preferred to remain
        silent
or of the ambassador, at once grave and sparkling,
from a country whose policy is to remain as relaxed as possible.

Part II

The Lake

1.

The lake
is shaped like wind.

2.

The body of it
persistent

as in the space
where a play was done
the arrangements of light.

3.

The rigged blooms
tied to their trellis,
the coils
and racks of filters.

Empty frame
where it happens.

4.

From the lake window
the wood noises came in
to say they went down
near the water
to gather the shapes of things.

5.

Gestures printed on air.

A spider-thread spiral
no longer inhabited by the gesturer.

6.

Like Chinese writing

it stoops down
where the breath starts

to stand in for grass.

7.

Five stalks
hesitant
in the black garden's
stubble carpet.

8.

To waver,
to be plucked,

to be twisted
pliable and grassy
out of rigor.

9.

Empty frame
where it happens.

The shadow players bent
one toward other
under suspended gauze.

A movement
as of stopped water.

10.

The lake
is shaped by wind.

11.

It uncurls in the cold.
All morning the furrows
repeat nothing.

12.

The tips of the furrows
seem to nestle
against what pushes them.

The Hill

1.

To bring the moon
Into place
Needs a wall and a fig tree.

2.

On the hidden hill
(Hidden because closed in)

They sit
On the wall under the fig tree.

3.

The skittish clouds
Abandon them to light.

4.

The philosophic night
Of shepherd and doctor

Strums the rubble
As if it were lute.

5.

Sky peels back
To prepare cold theater.

6.

Jump the wall: in the stretch
Of shadows a close party
Winds down, flares
By slaps and murmurs—
They got coins for ice—
Swung a lamp, it's
Doused.

7.

At the verge the gulch road
Barricades
Wind's tooth's gash

Save for a mouth
To haul brush up through
Or guard against refugees.

8.

There has been blood in the family,

Right in the center of the street
Where the roof covers it

The heads broken and emptied.

9.

They hunted them
Like wolves.

They covered the hills
Like hunters.

In the burning dawn
They jumped them like hunters.

10.

Often among alleys
Of dust trinkets
Walked heedless

In the shape of a refrain:
The citadel is my body.

11.

Brilliant silence
That from cliff scrapes frills

To scallop its chafings
For a ballad of trench-cuts:

By this the terrace
Is measured, and in its dips

And curtseys the hill's hidden
And bathed in cold rays.

12.

The black fig tree
Binds the mountainside.

Settlement holds captive
From flash flood.

The wall is a balance.

The naked moon
Chills to the bone.

In the blood-dark wine
They salute its ridges.

Late Geometric Grave-Offering

The glasses
Slipping from the head

And falling
From a great height

(Beyond guard-rail
Toward concealed walkway)

Will not be damaged
By the ancient stone wall

On whose top they land,
Cushioned

By tiny yellow blossoms,
A carpet of them—

The blossoms cling to the lens
Like dewdrops or newhatched spiders—

A veil the road
Glows gold through.

   ~

Eye-gleam
To ash

By spiraling
Ratchets.

The field
Falls

Into field,
Horizon

Snaps shut
On horizon.

~

Of the descent
Of the gleam,

Its dispersal
And loss of memory

Of kitchen light,
Breeze shift, pressure

Of hand where
Wrist was.

Of the journey
Of the gleam

Through layers of registry.
Of markings.

~

Twist of thread.

Twist of lettered
Thread.

Witness of withered,
Of witherer.

A torn page
With sketch of farm-hoardings,

Silo dome
In wet light

It seems to dangle from,
Swept in a stream

Of muddied shavings
That have numbers

And are not numbered.
A story in the wash.

        ~

There are notches
In the thread,

Stoneware balconies
The play of bathers

Is seen from
Or where through cleft

In black rock
The smoke trail

Pulls. Thinning
Tenuous backdraft

Seasoning what has already fallen.
Smoke going the wrong way in time.

        ~

Screw-head whorls
Toward the vanishing point

Of what it opens—
Well

From which the key
Was drawn up

Hidden in bucket
Toward blinding noon.

~

Padded with hours
Where buses go

And puddles
Where smoke leaks

Small dawns uncurl
And fold in the pockets

Of that place whose walls
Are flame roads.

The bright cups
Dash their gems out

Against the night—
Playing cards.

A field for a lake,
Two horses for a lion.

The green lady
Clears the table

With her air of secrecy.
Hymn to life,

Hymn to death.
A reversible sweater.

    ~

The radiant ziggurat
Pulses around its center.

The levels
Dance without touching.

Alpha wave
Of the dead.

A godhead
Made of sandblasted concrete.

Unstructured
Diamond.

    ~

Sheetmetal sunrise.
Bird archaeology.

Pileup as of cars
In fog.

Every word an adjective
Modifying the only noun,

That whose skin
Bruises in harbor air.

～

Before he has almost
Stopped looking

How the hill goes
And falls away from itself

Makes for a history
Of gulfs and folds.

How hell goes
And falls deeper into itself

Before
He has almost stopped looking

Makes for a history
Of glass and gold.

～

Drawn
To carved foam

Heat feeds
On stone flowers,

Crag-buds
Scratchy

After dust-cloud's
Rubdown.

～

The labyrinth is flat.

At the cusp of the construction site
Trance music
From the Noise Club.

Over the meadow of fresh cement
The wind blows dark.

～

"Put it down
In whole pieces"

—The pack,
Where the river starts,

Ready for transport.
They neglect sunlight here

Or disparage its brilliance.
Fit cracks of it

In tubes
That travel around corners—

She seems to walk
Through time—a figure

Escaping through the city
From the ancient bedroom.

～

Fragment
Of blue curl—

The whip
Or stem

That filled out
A lost splash—

Shines
Under broken glaze.

~

They sent ideas for crockery
Back and forth along the sea roads,

Came back with new ratios,
Slightly bulkier leaves

Or monkeys
Drunk on sun-glare.

~

Nothing
Chokes off

The flow of blue
Making monkey

Of red
Making tree

For monkey
To be lost in—

~

It wants to persist

A charred space
Left hollow for dancers—

Trench fretted
With blinking zigzags—

That opens and closes
In the same moment.

The Marsh

(for Armand Schwerner)

As soon as a name forms
It starts to burn
It starts to flake off

A strip of plank
Already folded in horn or cowl shape
A fold already splitting

Into wrecked forest
Its ground sheared
To be the sun's runway

The shape of a shout
Is the shape of a gulf
In the country whose ink pools

Preserve as if lovingly
What is flung in them
So that a fisher

Lost along a parallel branch
Beyond sight of bend
Might yet hope to tackle

Map-scrape or sunken clue
Clotted in the banks the rapids
Drag him between

~

There is the mark the
Bristle that crumbles
If air so much as kiss it

On a marsh of drafts
Lit by flares
There is the rumble

Of voices splitting scattering
Along the surface of the waters
A shout in shape of bristle

A bristle in shape of flame
A flame in shape of tongue
A tongue in shape of exploded star

The Deluge

(musique d'enfance)

SCENARIO: *While a group of adults listens to piano music at a private recital over the course of an afternoon in the late 1950's, a 10-year-old boy reads a lurid paperback novel—alleged to have been written by Leonardo da Vinci—about a great flood leading to the end of the world.*

1.

Splendor of doom
Hidden in a despised book

Works out its sentences
While the others smoke and talk

Of rates and stations
The programs for curtains

For which appointments are made
Even as the wave advances—

The piano music extends
Toward the porch,

He parts the curtain
And peers into the immense alcove—

Even as the wave advances
To engulf harbor life

And drown even the library
In which the book is buried.

2.

Naked in villas
Remote from plague

They part the curtains
To watch the hills for smoke.

Doves settle on pianos
In warning.

The message comes
(Across the hills

Through the open curtain)
Of the red sky that resembles a lady

Who rips the sky apart
Or is ripped apart by the sky—

She rode in on poison cloud
Glittering and splendid—

The message breaks off
Just as her face

Is about to break
Into speech.

3.

Evening lands.
We failed

Or were failed
So that the cities

In being erased
Might yield

Light's show,
The purple drift

Of her hand
Through glass stem

She holds
Out on the porch,

A clasp
To leave no mark

When the sky
Begins its change.

4.

Families of waves
Broken on the rocks

Register from the porch
As a howling

Of broken babies,
Bloodied breasts

Torn away in the storm.
In the harbor visited

By black wind
The books in the railed tower

Tear off
Page by page.

5.

Smoky stations
And programs for talk—

Middle of the opera—
The others drilled holes,

Built a world
For maps to crack open in.

Hatbox of pinups
Of theater gods,

The naked fountains
Soaked in wool smell,

Has opened
Since the beginning of time

Only to be sealed
As the opera shuts off.

6.

All afternoon
The world was ending.

The piano music—
A stream of dilated trills—

Has been telling of exiles
Whose velvet and mirrors

Can extend only until
The message breaks off.

They grew old in shadow,
When the waves came

They had forgotten
Even how to look out.

7.

The heroes
Are unraveled into poisoned sages—

Can only die naked
As coda of trill angles

Or faceted shard
On porch edge—

Who danced in the garden
Among trees of messages,

The gowns spangled with stars
And the women clasping glasses

In the purple drift
Of the hill light.

8.

He never even wrote
The book whose last sentence

Explained why the music party
Had to be interrupted

So that they could live in dread
Of clouds.

All afternoon
The day was ending.

They will startle,
Look up to see the purple

Of the curtains
Just being drawn.

9.

The bodies
Crumble into fabric,

A downward dance
Of stars

Dissipating
To their inner colors

Cool blue and yellow.
The pond is made of spaces.

The history of bodies
Is written with hedges and bouquets,

A field
For lamps to play on.

The pond is made of shadows.
When he saw them fall

The dancers
Entered the waves.

Part III

Songs Done In Praise of Winter

1.

If you could have invented
the doctrine of the ancient heretics

you would have,
and done it better.

The initiate rehearsing
for the ascent toward the cloud-hidden

meditates on the vein-lines of plaited fibers
and the undershades of crushed red petals.

The powder is scattered
so as to designate chapters.

At the reversed gate
with prayer beads and seedlings

you mark out a trail.
At its limit the dark god murmurs.

The thread as it uncoils
drapes its own windings

whose shadows
are scarred with fire.

2.

Sky
rolled up
in its darkness, not a puff
of wind, the letters
of a name sewn together
so it cannot be uttered.
The not yet created
sea
feels out
its mineral beds
and through the blind length
of its currents
dredges for islands.

3.

Friend, you know that girl
who by starlight picks buds
and simples on the mountain?
I thought it was her footstep
in the middle of my dream.

Must have been some other
late-night straggler,
not her, so surefooted
that when she walks in the dark
not even a pine needle snaps.

4.

She walks in
and the glass breaks
in his hand

scattering water
in the noon light.
He's struck still

vibrating in place
like the hummingbird
in the garden

lost in a trance
of overlapping petals.

5.

Hard to speak
cut down the middle:
I'd need
my other half

to finish saying this,
but it's beyond reach
still smoldering
from when the lightning struck.

6.

In the north country
    suns melt
        in red lakes.
A slow fog noses
    bluffs and of cliffs
        makes burrows.
Harp of maelstrom.
    Tree eaten by bird.
        When the land cracks open
water pours through the wounds.
    The slope
        floods against its crater
and in the blanket
    of snapped pine
        the knobs bud.

7.

From the time the mariachi band
went into its slow refrain
at the desert's edge

I can't remember a thing.
They call it cabin fever.

Nothing to do but listen
until the bush birds
suspend their noise

as a signal that the fugitives
can stop waiting for sunup.

8.

Ferry passengers disembarking.
Where are they going
where the bay brakes
on its carpet of scarves.

Where do they go
among the oil pools
and shelves of bells
where the harbor spills its parcels.

They are let go
toward cloaked ramps.
In the empty exit
the nets hang in coils.

The street unwinds
like a tripped spring.
They go where the dark
drips from between their fingers.

Sonic Ode

—scrim,
   a scroll
      thinned
         past shimmer
of fabric of cloth-
   of-rain, webstuff,
      lucent map
         of flat raked lakefront
hardly with planks enough
   to hold itself aloof from,
      weightless passenger
         in flight over dune zone's
cumulous fibrous
   whorls and resins,
      loops of pools,
         the nibbled rips of
folded cove forms,
   moss shore woven
      of murmurs spilt, split
         where Italic Diana
(her old priest struck down
   by her new priest)
      soaks up worship
         from the ground she abandons,
tufted colony
   in whose pillows her servants
      at play with the forest
         throw stones into time
miming for a theater
   of underbrush a comedy
      of bristle and vine,
         of solo leaf shudder
where unseen throat
   twines cries among thorns
      and spines, where choric
         chatter of chirp-creaks

flickers like lost chunks
        of light between brambles
                as medicine among rocks
                is scooped up mutely,
and the rays are splintering,
        the hill
                where the hunter clambers
                holds platform
for goat masks, they puncture
        the mountain for flute vents,
                smear the roof
                with hunt scenes,
to find past the curtain
        a succession of curtains,
                bud net, bead stream,
                vase for shades,
a strand of stains
        where tracks are melt marks,
                melody markers,
                catches
for shards of arches,
        opening around chasm-flanks,
                the fringes tumbled outward,
                as cases of faces
spilled in wind, tipped
        in sting of spin, a pin span
                snapped, its scar
                a harbor hub, a babble
of bent coin, lane hammers,
        tram gone groggy,
                hagglers in ash paths,
                porch covers, pockets of
crowds shrouded in houses,
        sleep cops, ticketmakers
                slapped up in gauze,
                disappearing cities
yanked blind toward
        thread's end, toward

                crack of blind
                    where bauble trebles
        to fen gleam, fan transit,
            smoke-dwelling alchemist
                    in crocodile jacket
                        and blue-beaded salamander
        hat proposing
            (coiled) a grid
                    of cloud-braids, mud-born
                        amulet in whose ambit
        gods ride twin snakes
            toward the capital of rain,
                    gods slide in flakes,
                        stacks of popped bubbles
        (making like chips
            in mid-flip) to excavate
                    bounce, paddle
                        the tatters in a remnant
        of dip, flume where
            the river combs its thickets,
                    the figure roams its fidgets,
                        tones its littles, its withs,
        till it tips off a half
            of baked crag, hefted
                    wedge of tithes, to go drop,
                        let coat fall,
        hat roll, mat spool
            on hall wall, signal
                    from rudimental radio,
                        fathom of blanket,
        breeze dragged
            over nerve reef,
                    tongue loops doubled
                        as gong echo, pouch
        in which storms are smuggled,
            sea scraped of rigging,
                    hold of black folds
                        dropped around space house,

aired-out tree
      in its flight body, a hollowed
         chord scoured
            by the flame of the flame,
a term of generative
      grammar, a term limit,
         liminal and grainy,
            scoured by the refrain
of the flame song, hauled
      through the track of the rake,
         a chip of ash-flake
            wedged against the grate,
ground by wind
      into powder, into parts
         of speech, torn nouns,
            sandtracks of verbs,
   pauses in shore pulse,
      water poured through water,
         sky raked free
            of clouds, sky
scrubbed between mountains
      over and over
         until the light
            squeaks—

Sonic Coda

The scene opens in a mountain where a lake
Frequented by helicopters is compared to a curtain
Stretched across the screen of a glamorous fake-
Babylonian movie palace. Increasingly uncertain
Of their location, the lovers as they prepare to embark
On an unscheduled holiday tell stories about the dark

Mythologists who provided material for a game
Of symbolic violence, changed by impromptu grace
Into playful sculptural ornament. The aim
Is to alter the nature of time, within a space
Which is altered also. All things in the yard
Get new names: sun's pond, and stone is card.

When they laugh the aftereffect resembles a hill
On whose brow medicinal herbs in spiked clusters
Glisten. Hunters perform a drama: The Kill.
It establishes the basis for a barbaric art form, musters
Crowds into amphitheaters carved out of natural settings
Where they watch human crises unfold like fans or jettings

Of water or crazy rock scrawls. Here everything blends,
Shadows resemble containers, and threads are often mistaken
For roadways that on closer approach turn out to be the bends
Of canyons from whose foam bath further noises awaken,
The blare of car jams, factory ramps, shopping centers thick
With nervous crowds of buyers and inspectors until a trick

Of light shrinks all to lightbulb size. A god in a mask
Steps out of the smoke and sets off riding with his twin
On a cloud made of what they turn back into when they ask
For a quick drink, a bunch of alphabet blocks taken from a bin
And scattered across the rug. In a hammock to watch a palm
Turn reddish in dusk light becomes a way to define the calm

Authority of major storm systems. As if sound were flame
The tune feeds on the notes that vanish in being sounded
And in turn is consumed by the air into which its name
Is translated simply by causing a word to be surrounded
By silences and letting the silences relax into a hedge
Against the wildness that flowers wherever a structure meets its
    edge.

Tree of Names

Vein-in-the-trail
Cactus
Whale-spine

Seam-in-the-seed
Axis
Tundra

Lane-for-thunder
Basin
Loop-slap

Knot-knits-core
Table-rock
Stem

Root-drags-twine
Thorn-shoulder
Gap-hoot

Herd-of-yodels
Winged-thicket
Bundle

String-hung-with-ditches
Fringe-that-hums
Furrow

Fire-in-the-hand
Tongue-forest
Sky-rope

Hill-hanging-down
Dangling-gate
Flecked-ledge

Chopped-up-river
Bark-peeled-loose
Blind-road

Flame-gone-black
Alley-for-noise
Ground

Providence

He built a poem
In such curious wise
That the reader might bury things
Among the words of its lines

Just as the provident traveler
Puts bread into a pouch
Or a child slides under floorboards
The image ripped from a forbidden book.

What the reader hid
Lay imperceptible under the surface
Like a weapons cache planted in the desert
By the harbingers of an invading army.

The sand looked exactly like sand.
The blue leaked blue continuously.
The poem appeared to be the formal description
Of an ancient and disheveled garden

Whose patterns of irrigation
Congealed at a more recent date
Into abstract vinelike loops
Sporadically torn or blotted.

It was never clear if the hole
In the lower right corner of the stanza
Was the remnant of a tomb door
Or the path to the picnic area.

The words only said: "It dampens,
And just as fringes hang from a branch
The response of an apostate servant
Rattles in the cavelike morning."

Years later the astonished reader
Opens to the forgotten page
And recoils from the still-visible
Contour of a painful slash

He had blotted formerly
Against the refrain that contained "vines."
In place of what was written
("Cork's odorous fetch" or "the split altar")

He studies as if under duress the map
Of a wound—complete with nerves and ornaments—
Exact as when the poet teased it
From the wallpaper of a vacated room.

The Ring

On either side of noon
the bodies measure their shadows.
We lose track of ourselves
only in the play of light,
variable and singular,
its arching and dissolving
our ligature to the rhythm
by which the green darkens
and loses its edges,
or the sill dust
glistens at the first ray.
To the end of the rug,
that tangled fringe,
is as far at times
as understanding can venture.
These must be cliffs,
wave-eroded, that have borrowed
the form of thread-tips.
The tufted foam
splashes against air
and air splashes back.
To belong to nothing—
to be detached in sight of islands—
light makes such promises
as casually as it discovers
the blots and splinters
the rooms seem almost made of.
We can believe it embraces us,
that to pick up the alternating
cadence of gleam and shade
is to be rocked by it deliberately,
that to see is to be noticed,
or (believing nothing)

we can stretch as if to imitate
by a dance movement the shifting
of luminous apertures.
We wake to relive the origin of ballet.
Knowing how to move
is to remember having dreamt
of lucid works (the lovers contriving
a migration from their cave,
the mixed cascade of paints and plants,
the arrival of the messenger
and the decoding of his looped ropes
into rules for abandoning the floodwall)
which may come to exist
by virtue of unflexing the hand.
We make our territory a ring
for plain dance. The patterns
of movement are flat like sky,
with nothing to mirror them.
The ring of drops
on stone trembles twice,
once for echo,
once for echo's memory.
The sun burns in the water.
We tell stories about angles,
crevices, shelves.
We tell stories about stories.
From the disappearing hours
we salvage time enough
to translate, to find equivalents,
to touch, to uncover, to open the eyes
by closing them or close them by opening,
to find what is not here
in the heart of what is, to slide,
to be happened upon, by what trick
of replenishment to coax out
or undo, to lose or to learn how
to want to lose, to be
for once, at once, undone.

We become nothing
for as long as it takes
a curtain to billow
in a three o'clock breeze.
The cloth flaps back.
We are the history of weather.
We imagined a language
that could say what it is.
We imagined a music
that wouldn't disappear,
without having to worry
about where beats come from.
Everything we imagined
was already here. Poetry exists,
it was so close we almost missed it
until we noticed
we were made out of it.
There is no escape from saying.
It has the air
of making things simple.
Poetry exists. There is no escape
from the end of saying.
The wave forgets the shore,
the shore forgets nothing
as it guards the shape
of what overwhelms it.
The ring has no beginning
on either side of noon.

The End of the Year

1.

Impossible to remember
what is happening right now:
the pool that opens,
the bird
that calls out in warning.
At every step the ground bristles.
Impossible to recognize
the song whose echo it guards.

2.

Pool, in haze
you've glistened.
Caught by sun
a sliver of surface
pierced mist.
Lie there,
as if waiting.
To move
is to be overtaken.

3.

Recollect if you can
in what opera the window
opens a crack
to let the captive's song
fill the empty hall she's barred from.

In every opera.

Every opera
is moving now toward an end
that under the weight of its scenery,
its complement of drapes and horn players,
comes to resemble destiny.

4.

Outside the window
the city has been assembled
while you slept.
Its harbor
shudders with supply trucks.
From the vents of its towers
a sustained drone of air
rushes to fill the void that surrounds them.
For purposes of tunnel construction
clipped sirens—safety devices—
sound at unsystematic intervals.

(So, to the unopened window.
Pauses, scratches behind one ear.)

5.

(And in reply:)

You hacked parks, and furtive streams,
admire how langorous the scaffolding
aspiring to shuffle off its planks.

Be bright streak, bolt
tattooed on parade-ground
as signal that the sun wants to come back.

Build from nothing.
Build nothing,
until it's habitable.

6.

There has been a day
when light met shadow
and each forgot its nature.

At the core of that amnesia
the world remembered itself so well
that the day is not yet over.

Never stop continuing to forget
so that at the marriage of light and shadow
the guests may feast even in silence.

7.

"Westward the eye strays,"
a harbor song

badly translated
into opera libretto language.

Westward
my eye,

having strayed,
stays. "You must be my

soul sister,
soul sister,"

a stranger sings
in the Financial Center.

8.

But this is our story,
don't you remember?

How hard it is
to go.

How hard it is
to go further

than cities permit
even in the rooms

they lease grudgingly
to freelance composers

of partially completed operas.
By the time the song takes shape

it has become a protest
against conventional stage design.

9.

As I sprawled in X shape
bathing
in light reflected off ice

I thought I heard
a chorus of sirens, mezzos,
predicting a future

I had forgotten
since the beginning of time.
In that uncatchiest of songs

colors were sounds, thoughts
rug samples, and events
a form of experimental harmony,

puzzling like the dynamics
of a bubble chamber, yet not
beyond all conjecture.

10.

Sun-up.
Blank book.
The wheel

we fall from.
Woke among beads,
ripped atlases,

letters of mark.
"We went there,
it was winter, the ice

was a museum
from whose bare glassy branches
we plucked our wishes

and held them up
in front of each other
smiling, amazed."

11.

Sudden as an e-mail at midnight from the Antipodes
the harpsichord music breaks from its order

to land in a new key. The sound-sprinkler
strews water in loops and spools

so that the spaces between them
inscribe your name

as it would look if, watered
by music, it grew out of the ground.

12.

More names pile up in the corridor
than there is luggage to put them on:
Bosphorus, Canessa, Argo, Delancey.
He is permitted to wait
on condition that he read, in the waiting room,
all that has been left there, the records of feuds
over unpaid tribute, the War of the Poets,
the cargoes withheld or requisitioned,
down to the waiting lists themselves
even if finally they will be thrown away.
Now that the lights are out—he waited so long
that the others went home—the piles of magazines
become unreadable. He sits impatient
in a frayed armchair, with names for companions.

13.

A cup,
not worshipped,
merely abandoned.

A tiny cup kept
free of dust in a box,
and then discarded.

How hard it was
to let go of,
on the porch of the old house

by the railing
by the black pond.
There is a cup

that falls into the dark,
and all he can do
is tell me about it.

14.

Scratch-music
for the neolithic yard party.

Band of black,
band of ochre.

The body is made
of rugged rings.

Slash-marks looped
into divertimenti

show how complicated
the sky is

even when it's empty,
especially when it's empty.

15.

Filigree. Move the lamp. His sister
pours the cup. Thunder. They try
not to look at each other. Souvenir
of Thailand. A thin wrist. Everyone clusters
around the orange sofa. Thirty years.
Moon. Stained fur. An alto solo.
Forgot to call. What look like ruins
under street lamps. Monday. The handbag.
Scattered keys and pills. Polaroid
of the northern river. The shoulders
seen from behind. Motionless.
Almost motionless. At the far end of the rug
between them the room seems to tilt
into darkness. Almost forgot to call.

16.

When I was sixteen
mise-en-scène really mattered.
Framing—the way Otto Preminger
or Kenji Mizoguchi might line up lights
and people and furniture, and then move
the camera even while the people moved,
perhaps in contrary spirals—the complexity
and precision and emotional force of all that
seemed like the most important thing in the world.

Now on planet Fox or planet Shochiku
the beautiful ghosts still walk
even while the celluloid that held them decays,
whether it matters or not.

17.

In the dark
lit by gold-light
that dragons guard

the illuminated cousins
meet to share dream-flesh.
They came so far

to be here.
Having tasted
dragon's blood

they are drunk
on the secret meanings
of bird-song.

18.

Combed strand.
Stranded comb.

Haloed dune.
Folded span.

Rock lip.
Tide fan.

Speckled pleat.
Bottlecap oracle.

Nacre.
Mica.

Toned keen.
Horned fern.

19.

Fishing net,
or spider's web.

Somebody else's life
at one remove.

She wakes and drives
to the beach as if in a movie

in another part of the web.
We inhabit the domain of tension.

It gives, it twangs back
like a bent bow,

it never breaks. At one remove
somebody else

continues to feel her way
along the strand.

20.

Words, go where you find her,
in bed or in the reading room.
If she went to the beach
go to the beach. Offer yourselves to her,
let her take her pick from among you:
take green or gold as it pleases her,
baskets of colors, galaxies spread out like scarves,
the roll of hills imitated by lutes and hand drums.
Here's breeze. Here's blossom. Here's gong
fading over water. And what you can't bring,
what even all of you together can't say,
let her guess from the pauses between,
from the way you fall back one by one into silence.

Part IV

Fires Were Started

To wait on line for air
in the jammed lobbies
of the assaulted city,

to be cut off by smoke,
in the crush to lose sight of one's family,
to be unable to say goodbye:

the fire burns all night long
in the main concourse
of the dream and by morning

has reduced to cinders
even the names
and even the letters of the names.

(DREAM NOTATION, NEW YORK 1998)

A History

1.

In the middle of drinking wine
and of studying the curve
of the companion's shoulder,
curve defined by angle and her distance
from the light source, in the middle
of the middle—

2.

Afterwards
there will be the memory
of the exploded room,

a space of perfect freedom.

3.

They had forgotten what city they were in.
So temperate the day
they had forgotten almost their names
for as long as it took the sun,
shifting from faucet
toward the casual heap of cotton and leather,
to catch a zigzag stitch.

4.

Woke to the taste of ashes.

5.

The ancient world
of breached walls and famine tactics—
spies who hid in the gully—
they were living in it
and surrounded by it.
The position of the city in the river.
From those moorings
they traced a history of unladed bolts
of silk, stacks of etched boxes.
Wet stones, an air of arrival.

6.

The ancient world
of stolen glimpses. Outriders
describe the shapes of things.

Bulked masses,
what light hits from a distance.

The ancient world of borders.

7.

"And if I could invent
the air of that room, spin it
out of myself

like the gold thread in the story,
the room
to be made a permanent resort,

its windows guarded, and point of entry
hung with ornament—

what days would be celebrated,
festivals of breath
not written in any history—"

9.

A piece of wall
having had time to lose its markings
is border. Market in another city,
shored up by eroded diggings.

The wall ends
where something ended
to make place for river light
shifting through the accumulated passages.

One city resembles another
as one day resembles another,
as one face resembles itself
in an altered light.

10.

The room.
A view of buildings and water.

(PARIS SEPTEMBER 11–NEW YORK OCTOBER 5 2001)